MILLARD *Fillmore*

Millard *Fillmore*

OUR THIRTEENTH PRESIDENT

By Gerry and Janet Souter

SPIRIT
of America™

The Child's World®, Inc.
Chanhassen, Minnesota

7

MILLARD *Fillmore*

Published in the United States of America by The Child's World®, Inc.
PO Box 326 • Chanhassen, MN 55317-0326 • 800-599-READ • www.childsworld.com

Acknowledgments
The Creative Spark: Mary Francis-DeMarois, Project Director; Elizabeth Sirimarco Budd, Series Editor;
Robert Court, Design and Art Direction; Janine Graham, Page Layout; Jennifer Moyers, Production

The Child's World®, Inc.: Mary Berendes, Publishing Director; Red Line Editorial, Fact Research;
Cindy Klingel, Curriculum Advisor; Robert Noyed, Historical Advisor

Photos
Cover: White House Collection, courtesy White House Historical Association; © Bettmann/CORBIS:
14; Courtesy of the Buffalo and Erie County Historical Society: 12, 13, 15, 16,19, 30, 31, 33, 34, 35;
© Corbis: 7; The Library of Congress Collection: 6, 16, 20, 21, 22, 23, 25, 29, 32; Stock Montage: 9, 28

Library of Congress Cataloging-in-Publication Data
Souter, Gerry.
    Millard Fillmore : our 13th president / by Gerry and Janet Souter.
       p. cm.
    Includes bibliographical references and index.
    ISBN 1-56766-838-0 (lib. bdg. : alk. paper)
    1. Fillmore, Millard, 1800–1874—Juvenile literature. 2. Presidents—United States—Biography—
Juvenile literature. [1. Fillmore, Millard, 1800–1874. 2. Presidents.] I. Souter, Janet, 1940–   .
II. Title.
    E427 .S68 2001
    973.6'4'092-dc21
                                                            00-010569

14 21 33

Contents

Chapter ONE

From Poverty to Leadership

Millard Fillmore was considered a handsome gentleman in his time. His good looks and polite manner won him many friends. He also earned respect through hard work and determination to succeed.

MILLARD FILLMORE ROSE FROM LIFE AS A POOR farmer's son to become the 13th president of the United States. On January 7, 1800, Fillmore was born in a one-room log cabin in Cayuga County, New York. His father, Nathaniel, was barely able to scratch a living from the ground. Nathaniel and his wife, Phoebe, loved their son very much. They wanted him to have a better life. At the age of 14, they sent Millard to work as an **apprentice** at a cloth mill. There he would learn the craft of cloth making.

In those days, an apprentice agreed to work for very low pay for a certain length of time in order to learn a skill. To leave early, apprentices had to pay money to the boss as a penalty for not staying as long as they had promised.

To Millard Fillmore, the apprenticeship was more like slavery. He hated the work and the cruel mill boss who sometimes beat his workers. Fillmore saved what little money he made. He paid the penalty that allowed him to leave. Then he walked 100 miles back to his family's little cabin.

Fillmore's father refused to give up. He sent his son to work in a carding mill, where sheep's wool was untangled and spun into thread. The owner of this mill was a kind man. Fillmore learned to like the work. While tending the carding machines, he kept an open dictionary nearby. He would take a few minutes here and there to learn new words. He later remembered that he had been "determined to seek out the meaning of every word … which I did not understand … and … fix it in my memory."

The life of an apprentice was not any easy one, as shown in this 19th-century cartoon called "Sorrow of a Country Apprentice." Fillmore was determined to leave his apprenticeship. He saved every penny he could to buy his way out.

At age 16, Fillmore began attending a one-room school. A year later, using what little money he had, he subscribed to a circulating library. The library requested a small fee in exchange for loaning books to readers. Later a teacher in a nearby village started a school called the New Hope Academy. Fillmore enrolled and went to classes whenever he could leave the mill.

By 1819, 19-year-old Millard Fillmore was a handsome, strapping young man of six feet tall. He was in love with Abigail Powers, his 21-year-old teacher. She respected his **ambition** and his desire for education, and they became friends. But Fillmore was the son of a poor farmer. Abigail was an intelligent, well-read parson's daughter. He wanted to improve his position in life before even thinking of marriage. Although his apprenticeship still had two more years to go, he again paid the penalty money to leave the mill early. Nathaniel Fillmore supported his son's ambition.

The family moved to Montville, New York, where Nathaniel became a tenant farmer for Judge Walter Wood. This meant that Nathaniel farmed land for the judge.

Fillmore fell in love with his lovely, red-haired teacher, Abigail Powers. They married in 1826.

He received either some of the crop or a small amount of money in return. In a short time, Nathaniel persuaded the judge to take on Millard as an apprentice clerk in his law office.

Millard Fillmore was typical of many young men who wanted to become lawyers. They usually were employed by law firms as clerks. For this job, a young man had to know how to read and write. All legal papers had to be copied by hand and then taken to a printer to be set in type. Clerks had to know where legal information was found in a law library.

Millard Fillmore faced a seven-year apprenticeship. Once again, he was tied to a difficult and cruel employer. Fillmore longed to be his own man. His ambition drove him to take a teaching job to earn extra money. Then he bought out the rest of his apprenticeship so the judge would give him full pay for his work. But Fillmore and Judge Wood did not get along. After they had a bitter argument, Fillmore resigned. Brokenhearted, he returned to working the plow on the family farm. Many years later, Fillmore remembered this part of his life: "It made me feel for the weak and unprotected and to hate the insolent tyrant in any station in life."

Fillmore was desperate to achieve something with his life. He journeyed to the growing town of Buffalo, on the shores of Lake Erie. In 1822, he joined a law firm as a clerk.

It usually took a student three years to finish law school. Fillmore completed his studies in less than two years through the sheer force of his will. He impressed his fellow workers as he continued to teach school and study law at the same time. At the recommendation of his employers, Fillmore began to practice law.

Fillmore's early struggles shaped him into a hardworking, determined man. He would always fight for the underdog, having been one himself for so many years. He fought to hold on to what he had achieved and hoped to fit in among the leaders of his day. His clothes were elegant. He spoke clearly and was serious and **conservative** in both his manner and opinions. Fillmore left behind his crude, country habits in the same way he replaced his rough cowhide boots with polished leather shoes. Although his law work was not brilliant or showy, it was accurate and won him many court cases. Fellow lawyers and Buffalo's leaders began saying, "If Millard Fillmore goes for it, so do I."

Fillmore was admitted to the New York State **Bar** as a lawyer in 1823. Then he surprised everyone when he left Buffalo to practice law in the small town of East Aurora. By opening an office in a small community, he could get the experience he needed. Fillmore was modest, and his achievements in Buffalo had not gone to his head.

With his law practice established, he married Abigail Powers on February 5, 1826.

Interesting Facts

▸ In Fillmore's time, there were few law schools. Few young people could afford law school or the many books that were needed. Most lawyers in the West or in the back-woods learned by reading law books on the job while they worked as low-paid clerks in law firms. This type of study was called "reading law."

▸ The term "bar" originally came from the railing in a court-room where prisoners stood with their lawyers to face the judge.

Fillmore's law office in East Aurora, New York, is shown at right. Fillmore moved to the small town of East Aurora to gain experience as a lawyer.

Her faith in his abilities encouraged him. She knew about the social graces of the day, such as knowing which fork to use at the dinner table, which clothes to wear, and which people were important to meet. Her manners helped him move further away from his backwoods past. This final polish to his image led to his entry into **politics.** In 1828, the same year that his son, Millard Powers Fillmore, was born, the lawyer from Aurora found himself elected to the New York State **Assembly.** He was backed by the Antimason **political party.**

12

Great Meeting!

DEMOCRATIC ANTI-MASONIC
YOUNG MEN'S
COUNTY CONVENTION.

POLITICAL PARTIES IN THE FIRST HALF OF THE 19TH CENTURY WERE NOTHING like those of today. Often, a single cause or belief could evolve into a political party. The Antimasons were organized simply to combat the Ancient Order of Masons, also known as the Freemasons. The Freemasons are a "secret society" that was founded in 1717 in London, England. Their rituals and actions are kept secret from nonmembers. To become a member, a man must be elected by other members. Women are not allowed to become Masons.

The Masons were originally formed to promote religious and moral ideas. But Antimasons believed the organization was an "invisible empire." They thought the organization had gained too much power in the United States because of the important men who belonged to it.

In 1826, a Royal Arch Mason named William Morgan threatened to tell the order's secrets. On September 12, he was kidnapped by members and then disappeared. Antimasons claimed the Masons had murdered him, but no one was ever convicted. Antimasons claimed the organization got away with it because it was so powerful.

Masonic members were at all levels of government and society. Although many famous men (including President George Washington) had been Masons, newspapers and churches fueled the Antimasons' claims. Fillmore distrusted any organization that put itself beyond the rule of the law, as the Masons often had done. He joined forces with the Antimasons. The Antimasons' single goal, to destroy the Masonic Order, was not strong enough to maintain a political party. By 1834, they had disbanded. Most members of the party joined either the Whig or the Democratic parties.

Chapter TWO

A Man of His Time

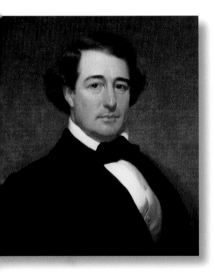

Fillmore quickly gained a reputation as a cautious and trustworthy man. This reputation earned him his first political office in the New York State Assembly.

FILLMORE WAS QUIET AND ATTENTIVE DURING his first term with the New York State Assembly in 1829. After his reelection in 1830, he took on more responsibility. He submitted a **bill** to keep people who could not pay their debts from being thrown in jail. It was passed in 1831, removing the shame of "Debtors' Prison." Always working for the "weak and unprotected," Fillmore was in favor of any increase in business that would provide more jobs. At the time, people and goods usually were transported on boats. People dug canals to create waterways across land. This made transportation from place to place both easier and faster. Fillmore backed bills to improve canals or dig new ones. Then, just as he became a force in New York State politics, he left public office in 1832.

Millard Fillmore's style of quiet leadership followed him into private life in Buffalo. Abigail gave birth to their daughter, Mary Abigail Fillmore. The family entered into Buffalo's social, **civic,** and political life. Fillmore helped draw up Buffalo's city **charter.** He saw to the creation of an organized fire-fighting system. The Fillmores enjoyed associating with Buffalo's **elite.**

By the end of 1832, Millard Fillmore was ready to enter national politics. The New York Antimasons elected him to the U.S. Congress that year. By this time, the Antimason Party was losing support. Fillmore urged them to disband and join the new Whig Party. The Whig political party was formed to oppose Andrew Jackson. As a hero in the War of 1812, Jackson was popular with the people. His years as president were riddled with **financial** uncertainty and panic, however.

Fillmore was quiet and observant during his first term in Congress, just as he had been

The Fillmore's daughter, Mary Abigail, was born in 1832.

when he entered the New York State Assembly. He gathered information by closely watching the actions of other lawmakers. Once again, he returned to private life in 1835 after serving only one term. But after a year spent in New York, he ran for office again. He was reelected to Congress in 1836.

During this term, Fillmore backed a high **tariff** on foreign goods that were brought into the United States. This was against the policy of President John Tyler, a southerner. High tariffs protected the sales of goods from the northern states. They made U.S. products

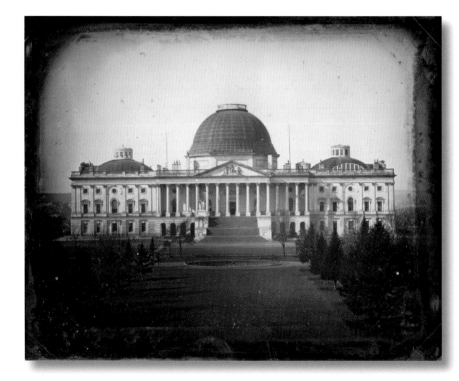

The U.S. Capitol building as it appeared during Millard Fillmore's first term in Congress. The short, turtle-shaped dome was replaced in the 1860s with the much taller one that remains today.

cheaper than foreign ones. But President Tyler supported low tariffs. They allowed necessary goods to come from Europe to the farming states in the South. Fillmore managed to delay votes until the government was desperate for money and needed the tariff payments. President Tyler was forced to sign the high-tariff bill into law.

The Whig Party was in the minority in Congress. Most of Congress belonged to the Democratic Party. The Whigs had to fight to get their laws passed. They had a difficult time making their opinions known because Democrats rarely let them have their say. Fillmore angrily challenged them, saying, "I speak by right, and not by permission! I will never … yield a right … guaranteed by the **Constitution."**

In 1844, Fillmore departed Congress once again—this time to run for New York State governor. He was beaten by a heavy **immigrant** vote in New York City against the **"nativist"** (anti-immigrant) Whigs. Many Americans who were born in the United States feared they would lose their jobs to the waves of foreigners who were pouring into the country.

Nativists believed "native" Americans—those who were already here working in government and business—should run the country. They wanted immigrants to hold only the lowest paying jobs. In fact, they did their best to stop immigration altogether.

In 1847, Fillmore was elected to the powerful job of state **comptroller.** He controlled the spending of New York's money. He and Abigail moved to Albany, the state capital. They sent their son to Harvard Law School and enrolled their daughter in a Massachusetts school for young ladies. Fillmore once again held an important state office. He would not stay out of national politics for long, however. The scramble for control of the **federal** government would soon pull him back to the nation's capital.

The United States had gone to war with Mexico in 1846. The Mexican War ended in early 1848, and the United States won a huge piece of land, known today as the states of California, Nevada, Utah, Arizona, and New Mexico. Americans had to decide whether the new territories would permit slavery.

General Zachary Taylor became a hero during the Mexican War. He had a **plantation** and owned slaves, which made him popular with Whigs from the southern states. The Whigs **nominated** Taylor as their presidential candidate. Now the party needed to find a candidate for vice president who would please antislavery Whigs in the North.

All attention turned to Millard Fillmore, and soon he was nominated to run with Taylor. The Whig **ticket** of Taylor and Fillmore won the 1848 election by a small number of votes. Once again, Fillmore packed his belongings for the move to Washington. This time, his wife was very ill and did not go with him. He would be without her advice and support as he started the most important job of his successful career.

Abigail and Millard's son, Millard Powers Fillmore, followed in his father's footsteps to become a lawyer. He attended Harvard Law School and went on to become his father's assistant in Washington, D.C.

19

A campaign poster features the Whig Party candidates for the 1848 election:
Zachary Taylor and Millard Fillmore.

IN 1845, THE U.S. GOVERNMENT CLAIMED TEXAS AS PART OF THE **UNION** and hoped to claim California as well. As Mexicans and Americans fought over these lands, many American citizens along the border were injured. Property was damaged as well. Finally, Congress declared war on Mexico.

On January 1, 1846, American troops under General Zachary Taylor crossed into Mexico. The territories that are now the states of California and New Mexico were occupied by U.S. troops. At about that time, the U.S. Navy cut off supplies that reached Mexico by sea.

The American army was victorious as it fought its way through Mexico. The Mexican government refused to admit defeat until the capital, Mexico City, fell in the autumn of 1847. The war ended with a U.S. victory and the **Treaty** of Guadalupe Hidalgo. This treaty gave the United States the land that would become the states of New Mexico, Nevada, Utah, Arizona, and California. By winning the war, General Zachary Taylor had become a great American hero.

Chapter THREE

"Zachary Taylor is no more"

President Zachary Taylor was a war hero, just as many other American presidents have been. But he was very inexperienced in politics. In fact, he had never even voted in an election. His presidency was a short one. He died after just 16 months in office, and Millard Fillmore became the 13th president.

WITH THE WHIG'S VICTORY IN THE ELECTION of 1848, Fillmore stepped into a political whirlwind. The Senate was equally divided between states that supported slavery and states that were against it. The new territories won in the Mexican War threatened to upset that balance. California's new constitution banned slavery, so the southerners rejected any bill including that **territory.** Northern **abolitionists** wanted slavery banned in all the new territories.

According to the U.S. Constitution, the vice president **presides** over the Senate. If any vote ends in a tie, the vice president casts the tie-breaking vote. It appeared that the difficult slavery issue was apt to stall with a tie. Fillmore knew he might very well have to cast the deciding vote. His northern supporters clamored for

As vice president, Fillmore presided over the Senate and would be called upon to cast a tie-breaking vote on the issue of slavery.

him to take their side, while the southern states threatened to **secede** from the Union and form their own country. Fillmore was torn.

During the presidential campaign, Fillmore had said that he was against the slavery of any human being. But he also believed the states, not the federal government, should decide whether to allow slavery. He said he regarded "slavery as an evil, but one with which the National Government had nothing to do."

Senator Henry Clay proposed a **compromise** in January 1850. California would be admitted as a free state in which no slaves would be permitted. New Mexico and Utah would be admitted as territories and allowed to make their own decisions about slavery. A slave market operated in the nation's capital city. Clay's compromise stated that the slave **trade** would not be allowed in Washington, D.C. Finally, the federal government would firmly enforce the Fugitive Slave Act of 1793. This act stated that any slaves who escaped to the North had to be returned to their southern masters. Clay's ideas became known as the Compromise of 1850. Senators argued angrily about these issues.

24

Fillmore was in a bad position. He did not want to cast the tie-breaking vote. As June 1850 approached, tempers were as hot as the summer weather that drove many congressmen from the capital city. President Taylor was against the Compromise bill. He threatened to **veto** if the Senate passed it. The Senate was in a panic. Everyone was waiting to see how Fillmore would vote.

Fillmore never cast that ballot as vice president. At noon on July 9, 1850, Fillmore

Congressmen from the North and the South bitterly debated whether slavery would be allowed in the new territories. Henry Clay (standing at center) proposed a compromise to Congress in 1850. He hoped it would hold the Union together.

was alone in the Senate chamber when a messenger informed him that President Taylor was seriously ill. Fillmore visited the president at the White House and then went to his apartment at Willard's Hotel. Late that evening, a messenger brought a note. There were many words on it, but he could only see the important ones:

"Sir, … Zachary Taylor is no more."

With the death of the president, Vice President Fillmore was required to take over. He was sworn in as the 13th president of the United States on July 10, 1850. He gave no speech at the **inauguration.** "Neither the time nor the occasion appeared to require [it]," said Fillmore. "The country was shrouded in … grief."

Fillmore did not sleep that night. His place in U.S. history depended on his next actions, and he was nervous. After heated discussions, the Senate accepted most parts of Henry Clay's Compromise bill. California became a state. Utah and New Mexico were admitted as territories and would decide their own slavery questions. Washington's slave market was closed. A stronger Fugitive Slave Act was passed. When President Fillmore signed the new act, it seriously angered those who wanted to see slavery ended. He saw it as an act of compromise to save the Union from a **civil war.** His northern supporters saw it as a betrayal.

Fillmore believed that both sides had misunderstood him. "In the North I was charged with being a pro-slavery man, seeking to extend slavery over free territory," he wrote, "and in the South I was accused of being an abolitionist. But I am neither." He had simply done what he believed was best for the Union.

On October 23, 1850, Fillmore wrote to Daniel Webster, one of his advisors. "God knows that I detest slavery," wrote Fillmore, "but it is an existing evil, for which we [the present government] are not responsible, and we must endure it, and give it protection as is guaranteed by the Constitution 'til we can get rid of it without destroying the last hope of free government in the world."

While trying to calm the North-South conflict, Fillmore tried to be an effective president between 1850 and 1852. His son became his secretary at the White House. His beautiful daughter and frail wife guided

Japan had been closed to trade with America and Europe for more than 200 years when Fillmore became president. Under a plan proposed by President Fillmore, Commodore Matthew Perry sailed into the closed port of Yeddo. This journey finally reopened Japan to trade with the United States.

the social life at the White House. He approved a plan for Commodore Matthew Perry to sail a small fleet to Japan. He hoped the voyage would open that country to American trade. In 1853, Perry sailed into the formerly closed port of Yeddo and began to **negotiate** an agreement.

During his time, Fillmore also proposed a transcontinental railroad, which was finally completed in 1869. Always avid readers,

Fillmore and Abigail installed the first library in the White House.

Fillmore had a vision for the United States. Future presidents acted on many of his ideas. His party chose not to nominate him for another election, so his term ended in 1852. Democrat Franklin Pierce was elected over the Whig candidate, General Winfield Scott. The Whig Party was finished.

Shortly after the Senate passed the Compromise of 1850, this portrait was made to honor the decision. Fillmore is seated at right, holding the shield. Henry Clay, who proposed the Compromise, is seated at center.

Chapter FOUR

Return to Buffalo

Abigail Fillmore caught a cold at Franklin Pierce's inauguration. She soon died of pneumonia.

THE WEATHER DURING FRANKLIN PIERCE'S inauguration was terribly cold. A bitter wind whipped through the nation's capital. But Millard and Abigail Fillmore stood by to honor the new president at the outdoor ceremonies. Unfortunately, Abigail caught a cold that quickly turned into pneumonia. She died later that month on March 30, 1853. Broken-hearted, Fillmore returned to Buffalo. A year later, tragedy struck again. His daughter died at age 22 after a sudden illness. The loss of his beloved wife and daughter crushed Fillmore.

Nonetheless, he continued to work for the good of his city. He helped found Buffalo General Hospital in 1855. He also became involved with a new political party, the "Know-Nothings." This group was officially

known as the American Party. It grew out of the anti-immigrant "nativists" of the 1840s. Although the American Party members were not strictly against immigration, they wanted to restrict the rights of newcomers. They did not believe immigrants should have the right to vote or hold public office. They also favored a 21-year waiting period before immigrants could become U.S. citizens.

Interesting Facts

▶ When people asked members of the American Party about its ideas and goals, they often responded by saying, "I know nothing." They wanted to keep their ideas secret, earning them the nickname of the "Know-Nothing" Party.

31

Fillmore's anti-immigrant feelings grew firm when immigrants in New York City voted against him in the 1844 election for governor. So when the American Party asked him to run for president in the 1856 election, he accepted. He was defeated by James Buchanan, who became the nation's 15th president.

Finally, Fillmore retired from political life. In 1858, he married Caroline McIntosh, a wealthy widow. During the American Civil War, he supported Buffalo's volunteer soldiers and the Union cause. He strongly criticized Abraham Lincoln and the Republican Party, however. He said they were too quick to go to war. He thought the North and South should have tried to negotiate first. Still, Fillmore stood firm with his country. At a meeting in Buffalo, he said, "My fellow citizens, it is no time for any man to shrink from the responsibility which events have cast

Caroline Carmichael McIntosh was a wealthy Buffalo widow with no children. Although Fillmore never planned to marry after Abigail died, he proposed to McIntosh in the late 1850s.

upon him. We have reached a crisis … when no man … has the right to stand **neutral.**"

Many of his enemies accused him of **treason** when he did not support President Lincoln. After Lincoln's death, Fillmore's house was splashed with black ink because he had not hung the traditional black **mourning** drape at the windows. As long as he lived, Fillmore stood by what he believed.

In February 1874, Millard Fillmore suffered a stroke, and on March 8, a second stroke killed him. Fillmore was truly an American of his time. He pulled himself up from his life as a poor farmer's son to become the vice president of the United States. He served as U.S. president for two difficult years while critics in northern states called him a **traitor** for signing the Fugitive Slave Act. But as the

To show his support for the Union cause during the Civil War, Fillmore organized a company of men who were too old to join the army. The group was called the "Union Continentals." Wearing uniforms of their own design, these men helped raise money for the war effort.

United States stood at the brink of civil war, he tried to preserve the Union. He lost his career in politics as he attempted to hold the nation together. Millard Fillmore was a civic leader, a respected man, and a master of compromise.

In 1858, Millard and Caroline Fillmore purchased an elegant mansion at 52 Niagara Square in Buffalo. He would live the rest of his life in that city, always involved in civic and social activities.

DURING THE SPRING OF 1862, BUFFALO CITIZENS WANTED TO FIND A WAY TO protect the "relics and records" of the city's colorful past. They approached Millard Fillmore to enlist his talent for organization. Less than 30 days later, the Buffalo Historical Society was founded. Fillmore became its first president. He threw himself into the work. At the opening ceremonies, he said, "the object of this society was not to study history … or for the formation of a library for that purpose; but its chief object is to collect and preserve materials of history relating to western New York, and especially Buffalo, for future use."

This limited goal was abandoned in a short time. Fillmore found himself both studying and teaching Buffalo history as the museum expanded. The society grew rapidly from its location at 7 Court Street (shown here), leasing rooms in other locations. Eventually, the society purchased the St. James Hotel in downtown Buffalo and remodeled it to house the Historical Society, the Fine Arts Academy, and the Society of Natural Sciences. Three of Fillmore's favorite institutions were now under one roof.

1800 Millard Fillmore is born on January 7 in a log cabin in Cayuga County, New York.

1814 Fillmore's father, Nathaniel, apprentices him to a cloth mill and wool carder.

1819 Fillmore meets Abigail Powers, his 21-year-old teacher. She respects him for his determination and ambition, and they become friends.

1822 Fillmore moves to Buffalo, New York, where he works as a law clerk.

1823 After being admitted to the New York State Bar, Fillmore becomes a lawyer. He opens his first law office in East Aurora, New York.

1826 Fillmore and Abigail Powers are married.

1828 The Fillmores' son, Millard Powers Fillmore, is born. Fillmore is elected to the New York Legislature. His term ends in 1831, and he does not seek reelection.

1832 The Fillmores' daughter, Mary Abigail, is born. Fillmore is elected to the U.S. Congress.

1835 Fillmore leaves Congress and returns to practicing law.

1836 Fillmore runs for Congress again and is reelected.

1844 Fillmore leaves Congress to run for governor of New York. He loses the election, in part because of the Whig Party's anti-immigrant stance.

1846 The United States goes to war with Mexico.

1847 Fillmore is elected New York State comptroller. In September, the United States captures Mexico City, forcing Mexico to surrender.

1848 The Mexican War ends with the signing of the Treaty of Guadalupe Hidalgo. The American victory adds new territories to the United States, including the region that would become the states of New Mexico, Nevada, Utah, Arizona, and California. The Whig Party nominates war hero Zachary Taylor as its presidential candidate. The party decides to find a northerner to run as the vice presidential candidate in an attempt to gain more votes. They nominate Millard Fillmore. Taylor and Fillmore win the election on November 7.

1849 Zachary Taylor is inaugurated as the 12th U.S. president on March 5. Millard Fillmore is the vice president.

1850 President Taylor dies in July after a brief illness. Fillmore becomes the 13th U.S. president. President Fillmore agrees to the Compromise of 1850 to help preserve the Union. By supporting the Compromise, he offends people on both sides of the slavery issue. The Compromise of 1850 admits California to the Union as a free state. New Mexico, Utah, and Arizona enter the Union as territories.

1851 President Fillmore proposes Commodore Matthew Perry's voyage to open trade with Japan. Perry does not set sail until 1853. President Fillmore also supports idea of a transcontinental railroad, which is completed in 1869.

1852 The Whig Party turns its back on Millard Fillmore and nominates General Winfield Scott as its presidential candidate. The Whigs lose the election, and the party falls apart.

1853 Franklin Pierce is inaugurated as the 14th U.S. president. Abigail Powers Fillmore attends the inauguration with her husband, although the weather is terrible. She catches a cold and dies of pneumonia.

1854 Fillmore returns to private practice and civic affairs in Buffalo. His daughter, Mary Abigail Fillmore, dies suddenly at age 22.

1855 Fillmore helps fund and build the Buffalo General Hospital.

1856 Fillmore runs for president as the "Know-Nothing" Party candidate. He loses the election to James Buchanan, who becomes the nation's 15th president.

1858 Fillmore marries Caroline McIntosh, a wealthy widow. They purchase a mansion on Niagara Square and frequently host parties.

1861 Fillmore supports the Civil War but is critical of Abraham Lincoln. Some people accuse Fillmore of treason because he does not support the president. To prove his support for the Union cause, however, Fillmore organizes a company of men who are too old to fight in the war. The group calls itself the "Union Continentals."

1862 Fillmore helps found the Buffalo Historical Society.

1867 Fillmore founds the Buffalo Society for Prevention of Cruelty to Animals.

1874 Millard Fillmore dies on March 8 of a stroke.

37

abolitionists (ab-uh-LISH-uh-nists)
Abolitionists were people who wanted to end slavery in the United States. Northern abolitionists felt that Fillmore did not do enough to end slavery.

ambition (am-BISH-un)
Ambition is a strong desire to succeed. Abigail Powers admired Millard Fillmore's ambition.

apprentice (uh-PREN-tiss)
An apprentice is a person who is learning a skill under the teaching of an expert worker. In Fillmore's time, an apprentice agreed to work for very low pay for a promised length of time.

assembly (uh-SEM-blee)
An assembly is a group of people gathered together for some purpose. Fillmore was elected to the New York State Assembly, which makes laws for the state.

bar (BAR)
A bar is a group of practicing lawyers. Lawyers in New York State belong to the New York Bar.

bill (BILL)
A bill is a proposed law presented to a group of people who make laws. Congress and the president decide if bills will become laws.

charter (CHAR-tur)
A charter is a written statement that grants certain rights to people or a group. Fillmore helped write the charter for the city of Buffalo.

civic (SIV-ik)
Civic means having to do with a city. Fillmore was interested in Buffalo's civic affairs.

civil war (SIV-il WAR)
A civil war is a war between opposing groups of citizens within the same nation. Fillmore hoped the Compromise of 1850 would prevent a civil war.

compromise (KOM-pruh-myz)
A compromise is a way to settle a disagreement in which both sides give up part of what they want. The U.S. Senate created the Compromise of 1850 in an attempt to satisfy both the North and the South.

comptroller (KOMP-troll-ur)
A comptroller is someone who keeps track of a company's or government's earnings and how much is spent. As the state comptroller, Fillmore could help decide how money was earned and spent for the state.

conservative (kun-SER-vuh-tiv)
If someone is conservative, he or she is cautious and prefers not to take risks. Fillmore was considered a serious and conservative man.

constitution (kon-stih-TOO-shun)
A constitution is the set of basic principles that govern a state, country, or society. California's constitution outlawed slavery.

elite (ee-LEET)
The elite are people who enjoy special privileges, often because they are wealthy and well educated. The Fillmore family was among Buffalo's elite.

federal (FED-ur-ul)
Federal means having to do with the central government of the United States, rather than a state or city government. Fillmore believed that individual states, not the federal government, should decide whether to support or reject slavery.

financial (feh-NAN-shul)
Financial means having to do with money or how it is used. During Andrew Jackson's presidency, the United States had financial problems.

immigrant (IM-uh-grent)
An immigrant is a person who moves from his or her homeland to a new country. New York City had a large population of immigrants from many foreign countries during Millard Fillmore's time.

inauguration (ih-naw-gyuh-RAY-shun)
An inauguration is the ceremony that takes place when a new president begins a term of office. Abigail Fillmore became seriously ill after Franklin Pierce's inauguration.

mourning (MOUR-ning)
Mourning is a deep sadness over the death of a person. People sometimes show mourning with a symbol or sign of sorrow, such as wearing black clothing. Fillmore did not hang a mourning drape at his home when President Lincoln was killed.

nativist (NAY-tuh-vist)
A nativist was someone who believed that immigrants should not be allowed to vote in elections or hold public office. Fillmore became a nativist after he lost an election because of a strong immigrant vote.

negotiate (neh-GOH-she-ate)
If people negotiate, they talk things over and try to come to an agreement. Commodore Perry sailed to Japan to negotiate a trade agreement.

neutral (NOO-trul)
If a people are neutral, they do not take sides. Fillmore believed that no one should remain neutral during the American Civil War.

nominate (NOM-uh-nayt)
If people nominate someone, they choose him or her to run for office. The Whigs nominated Fillmore to be their candidate for vice president.

plantation (plan-TAY-shun)
A plantation is a large farm that grows crops such as tobacco, sugarcane, or cotton. Zachary Taylor was a southern plantation owner and a slave holder.

political party (puh-LIT-uh-kul PAR-tee)
A political party is a group of people who share similar ideas about how to run a government. The Whig political party was a group of people that joined forces to oppose President Andrew Jackson.

politics (PAWL-uh-tiks)
Politics refers to the actions and practices of the government. Millard Fillmore's first job in politics was as a member of the New York State Assembly.

presides (preh-ZYDZ)
If someone presides over a meeting, he or she is in charge of it and must keep order during discussions. The vice president presides over the Senate.

secede (suh-SEED)
If a group secedes, it separates from a larger group. Before the Compromise of 1850, the southern states threatened to secede from the United States and form their own country.

tariff (TAIR-if)
A tariff is a tax charged to a foreign country when it brings its goods into the United States. The southern states used many products from overseas and wanted to keep tariffs low.

territory (TAIR-uh-tor-ee)
A territory is a land or region, especially land that belongs to a government. Utah and New Mexico were made territories of the United States.

ticket (TIK-it)
In an election, a ticket is the list of candidates from the same political party who are running for office. Zachary Taylor and Millard Fillmore were running on the Whig ticket.

trade (TRAYD)
Trade is the business of buying and selling things. The Compromise of 1850 made the slave trade illegal in Washington, D.C.

traitor (TRAY-ter)
A traitor is a person who betrays his or her country. People said Fillmore was a traitor when he signed the Fugitive Slave Act.

treason (TREE-zun)
Treason is the act of hurting one's country or helping its enemies. People accused Fillmore of treason when he refused to support President Lincoln.

treaty (TREE-tee)
A treaty is a formal agreement between nations. Mexico was forced to accept the terms of the Treaty of Guadalupe Hidalgo in 1848.

union (YOON-yen)
A union is the joining together of two or more people or groups of people, such as states. The United States is also known as the Union.

veto (VEE-toh)
A veto is the president's power to refuse to sign a bill into law. President Zachary Taylor threatened to veto the bill that became the Compromise of 1850.

Our PRESIDENTS

President	Birthplace	Life Span	Presidency	Political Party	First Lady
George Washington	Virginia	1732–1799	1789–1797	None	Martha Dandridge Custis Washington
John Adams	Massachusetts	1735–1826	1797–1801	Federalist	Abigail Smith Adams
Thomas Jefferson	Virginia	1743–1826	1801–1809	Democratic-Republican	widower
James Madison	Virginia	1751–1836	1809–1817	Democratic Republican	Dolley Payne Todd Madison
James Monroe	Virginia	1758–1831	1817–1825	Democratic Republican	Elizabeth Kortright Monroe
John Quincy Adams	Massachusetts	1767–1848	1825–1829	Democratic-Republican	Louisa Johnson Adams
Andrew Jackson	South Carolina	1767–1845	1829–1837	Democrat	widower
Martin Van Buren	New York	1782–1862	1837–1841	Democrat	widower
William H. Harrison	Virginia	1773–1841	1841	Whig	Anna Symmes Harrison
John Tyler	Virginia	1790–1862	1841–1845	Whig	Letitia Christian Tyler / Julia Gardiner Tyler
James K. Polk	North Carolina	1795–1849	1845–1849	Democrat	Sarah Childress Polk

Our PRESIDENTS

President	Birthplace	Life Span	Presidency	Political Party	First Lady
Zachary Taylor	Virginia	1784–1850	1849–1850	Whig	Margaret Mackall Smith Taylor
Millard Fillmore	New York	1800–1874	1850–1853	Whig	Abigail Powers Fillmore
Franklin Pierce	New Hampshire	1804–1869	1853–1857	Democrat	Jane Means Appleton Pierce
James Buchanan	Pennsylvania	1791–1868	1857–1861	Democrat	never married
Abraham Lincoln	Kentucky	1809–1865	1861–1865	Republican	Mary Todd Lincoln
Andrew Johnson	North Carolina	1808–1875	1865–1869	Democrat	Eliza McCardle Johnson
Ulysses S. Grant	Ohio	1822–1885	1869–1877	Republican	Julia Dent Grant
Rutherford B. Hayes	Ohio	1822–1893	1877–1881	Republican	Lucy Webb Hayes
James A. Garfield	Ohio	1831–1881	1881	Republican	Lucretia Rudolph Garfield
Chester A. Arthur	Vermont	1829–1886	1881–1885	Republican	widower
Grover Cleveland	New Jersey	1837–1908	1885–1889	Democrat	Frances Folsom Cleveland

Our PRESIDENTS

	President	Birthplace	Life Span	Presidency	Political Party	First Lady
	Benjamin Harrison	Ohio	1833–1901	1889–1893	Republican	Caroline Scott Harrison
	Grover Cleveland	New Jersey	1837–1908	1893–1897	Democrat	Frances Folsom Cleveland
	William McKinley	Ohio	1843–1901	1897–1901	Republican	Ida Saxton McKinley
	Theodore Roosevelt	New York	1858–1919	1901–1909	Republican	Edith Kermit Carow Roosevelt
	William H. Taft	Ohio	1857–1930	1909–1913	Republican	Helen Herron Taft
	Woodrow Wilson	Virginia	1856–1924	1913–1921	Democrat	Ellen L. Axson Wilson Edith Bolling Galt Wilson
	Warren G. Harding	Ohio	1865–1923	1921–1923	Republican	Florence Kling De Wolfe Harding
	Calvin Coolidge	Vermont	1872–1933	1923–1929	Republican	Grace Goodhue Coolidge
	Herbert C. Hoover	Iowa	1874–1964	1929–1933	Republican	Lou Henry Hoover
	Franklin D. Roosevelt	New York	1882–1945	1933–1945	Democrat	Anna Eleanor Roosevelt Roosevelt
	Harry S. Truman	Missouri	1884–1972	1945–1953	Democrat	Elizabeth Wallace Truman

Our PRESIDENTS

President	Birthplace	Life Span	Presidency	Political Party	First Lady
Dwight D. Eisenhower	Texas	1890–1969	1953–1961	Republican	Mary "Mamie" Doud Eisenhower
John F. Kennedy	Massachusetts	1917–1963	1961–1963	Democrat	Jacqueline Bouvier Kennedy
Lyndon B. Johnson	Texas	1908–1973	1963–1969	Democrat	Claudia Alta Taylor Johnson
Richard M. Nixon	California	1913–1994	1969–1974	Republican	Thelma Catherine Ryan Nixon
Gerald Ford	Nebraska	1913–	1974–1977	Republican	Elizabeth "Betty" Bloomer Warren Ford
James Carter	Georgia	1924–	1977–1981	Democrat	Rosalynn Smith Carter
Ronald Reagan	Illinois	1911–	1981–1989	Republican	Nancy Davis Reagan
George Bush	Massachusetts	1924–	1989–1993	Republican	Barbara Pierce Bush
William Clinton	Arkansas	1946–	1993–2001	Democrat	Hillary Rodham Clinton
George W. Bush	Connecticut	1946–	2001–	Republican	Laura Welch Bush

Presidential FACTS

Qualifications
To run for president, a candidate must
- be at least 35 years old
- be a citizen who was born in the United States
- have lived in the United States for 14 years

Term of Office
A president's term of office is four years. No president can stay in office for more than two terms.

Election Date
The presidential election takes place every four years on the first Tuesday of November.

Inauguration Date
Presidents are inaugurated on January 20.

Oath of Office
I do solemnly swear I will faithfully execute the office of the President of the United States and will to the best of my ability preserve, protect, and defend the Constitution of the United States.

Write a Letter to the President
One of the best things about being a U.S. citizen is that Americans get to participate in their government. They can speak out if they feel government leaders aren't doing their jobs. They can also praise leaders who are going the extra mile. Do you have something you'd like the president to do? Should the president worry more about the environment and encourage people to recycle? Should the government spend more money on our schools? You can write a letter to the president to say how you feel!

1600 Pennsylvania Avenue
Washington, D.C. 20500

You can even send an e-mail to: president@whitehouse.gov

For Further INFORMATION

Internet Sites

Read Fillmore's messages to Congress and locate links to other sites:
http://www.interlink-cafe.com/uspresidents/13th.htm

Visit Millard and Abigail Fillmore's house in East Aurora:
http://home.earthlink.net/~pock/home_mf.htm

Read a biography about Millard Fillmore:
http://members.aol.com/icecold966/Fillmore.html

Read Fillmore's letter to the Emperor of Japan:
http://web.jjay.cuny.edu/~jobrien/reference/ob54.html

Visit the Buffalo and Erie County Historical Society and the city of Buffalo:
http://intotem.buffnet.net/bechs/

Learn more about the Compromise of 1850 and other events leading to the Civil War:
http://www.loc.gov/exhibits/treasures/trm043.html
http://www.wwnorton.com/college/history/ushist/timeline/comp1850.htm
http://www.worldbook.com/fun/aajourny/html/bh115.html

Learn more about all the presidents and visit the White House:
http://www.whitehouse.gov/WH/glimpse/presidents/html/presidents.html
http://www.thepresidency.org/presinfo.htm
http://www.americanpresidents.org/

Books

Casey, Janet Clark. *Millard Fillmore: Thirteenth President of the United States.* Danbury, CT: Childrens Press, 1988.

Cleveland, Will, and Mark Alvarez. *Yo Millard Fillmore (And All Those Other Presidents You Don't Know).* Brookfield, CT: Millbrook Press, 1999.

Paulson, Timothy, and Darlene Clark Hine. *Days of Sorrow, Years of Glory 1831–1850: From Nat Turner Revolt to the Fugitive Slave Law* (Milestones in Black American History). Broomall, PA: Chelsea House Publishers, 1994.

Sullivan, George. *Mr. President: A Book of U.S. Presidents.* New York: Scholastic Paperbacks, 1997.

Index